# To Mother /

## Overcoming Stillbirth

To Mother An Angel: Overcoming Stillbirth

Editor: Twana Griffin

Book Cover: LaKeisha Kelly

ISBN-13: 978-1511994231
ISBN-10: 1511994231

Scripture references appear in the endnotes:

Hengeveld, N., 1993. *BibleGateway.* [Online]
Available at: www.biblegateway.com
[Accessed 2014, 2015].

Primary translations: King James Version (KJV), New King James Version (NKJV), New American Standard Bible (NASB), The Message (MSG), New International Version (NIV)

To Contact the Author:

Connect on Facebook, LinkedIN

# Dedication

To Charlotte Evelina Price

As I write this book, it has been over a year since your stillbirth. God told me to write about our experience because of its greater purpose. The fact is stillbirth is one of those medical complications that most doctors can't explain. It's even harder to explain when a mother carries her child full-term and stillbirth occurs.

Charlotte, I didn't hide you from anyone when I was pregnant. I will not hide the fact that I love you more than I could have ever imagined loving a child!

I miss you so much!

Mommy loves you – Always! We will see each other again – I promise!

XOXO

# Table of Contents

# Foreword

Almost 20 years ago, my husband and I joined a vibrant and spirit-filled church called Mt. Vernon Missionary Baptist Church in Indianapolis, Indiana. One bright light in their active Youth Ministry was a young lady who served as Secretary for the entire Sunday School department. She was a confident and mature teenager who conducted her duties with skill, anointing, and commitment. Many of us affectionately referred to her as "Sister Secretary."

This outstanding young lady maintained her faith and commitment to serve God through many tests and trials. She is now a beautiful woman with the life-changing testimony shared in this book.

Latonia's story is sure to encourage and inspire all who read it. As I read her story, I was amazed by her ability to keep her head up and fight though adversities that would have sidelined most of us. Because of her obedience and faithfulness, this book will bring healing, deliverance and peace to many.

I am convinced this is just the beginning of how God will use Latonia to advance His Kingdom. She is a true example of what it means to serve God faithfully. She has embraced the opportunity to serve women around the world by sharing her heart.

Prepare to experience a portion of Latonia's journey as she invites you into the intimate places of her life...The places where pain, confusion and sometimes despair have turned into an elevated level of faith, increased compassion for others and an even greater level of ministry and service.

Timeko Whitaker

Author, Speaker, Coach

CEO, Authentic Identity Coaching, LLC

www.authenticidentitycoaching.com

# Preface

*"When fetal death occurs after 20 weeks of pregnancy, it is called stillbirth. These tragic deaths occur in about 1 in 160 pregnancies. Most stillbirths occur before labor begins. The pregnant woman may suspect that something is wrong if the fetus suddenly stops moving around and kicking. A small number of stillbirths occur during labor and delivery."[1]*

I don't want to hide what happened. We read and see so much that happens to people but do we ever know the real story? Most people tell me I inspire them because I continue to live day by day, smiling and enjoying life. It didn't happen overnight but I've never been a person that liked to hide or admit defeat no matter the obstacles in my life.

The purpose of this book is to help encourage and strengthen parents dealing with stillbirth. While this book may be read by a wide audience of individuals, the people who will understand and appreciate it most are mothers and fathers who have endured the loss of their child.

Unfortunately, there is a stigma associated to stillbirth that I still don't totally understand. As I wrote this book and learned even more facts about stillbirth, I was amazed more stories are not being told.

Revelation 12:11 says *we overcome by the words of our testimonies.* Why don't more parents testify? Could it be they are convinced that losing a child, particularly a newborn, can't possibly be the good works of God? Since when does a testimony have to end the way we think it should – happily ever after?

The death of a loved one is never pleasant to experience but we accept it when it is a relief from suffering. I remember when my grandmother died from stomach cancer. I cried but I understood it was for the best. My grandfather died of lung cancer. I cried but I understood he wouldn't suffer anymore. My daughter was stillborn. I cried but I understood she didn't have to endure pain or obstacles in this sinful world. It was best for her according to God's Will.

I have learned that everything in God's Will is not understandable by the human mind. Stillbirth doesn't make sense, but it is still a part of God's perfect and divine Will.

I realize there are mental health professionals and documented grief recovery processes that people may need to follow. This book is not to replace those services but to serve alongside them to remind you – you are not alone in your experience.

I pray that as you read these pages you will be strengthened and encouraged to trust God even more.

End Notes

1 – http://www.marchofdimes.org/loss/stillbirth.aspx (March of Dimes Foundation, 2014)

# Acknowledgments

To God – all honor, glory, and praise belongs to you! Without you, I'm nothing more than an empty and lost vessel on this earth!

To my husband – I love you so much! Your spiritual strength often amazes me but I know you are chosen by God to be my covering. You have been and continue to be the greatest husband of all time! Thank you, Sweetie!

To all of my family – I love you all! You all love Charlotte as though she is still here! Thank you for loving me! To my in-laws, some people have horror stories about their in-laws. Whenever someone asks me about mine, I tell them you all are wonderful! Thank you, thank you, and thank you!!

To my pastor and wife, Bishop Larry D Grinstead and Janet Grinstead – thank you for being there for me and my husband. When this all happened, we hadn't really been at Puritan MBC for that many years but you all definitely showed a level of ministry and love that truly was beyond our expectations. Thank you!

To my friends – you all showed up and provided support when it really counted! Thank you!

To the readers who will read this book – THANK YOU!

# Introduction

When a woman becomes pregnant, most women realize that a miracle has happened. Women who are married and who have been trying for years know this all too well. For a woman with my health history, I knew it would be by God's hand alone that I would become pregnant. As a woman of faith, I knew if anyone could do it – God could!

However, I must admit the journey was tough at first. It was hard to deal with the disappointment of taking multiple home pregnancy tests with no positive signs. The constant praying and seeking God with the same questions. Will it ever happen for us? When will it happen? The fight to silence doubts and fears began to overtake my mind. This struggle caused more questions. Is there something wrong with me? Did I do something in my past that I now I have to reap the consequence of being barren? Is God saying we won't make good parents?

My husband and I did our best to keep our faith in God. We trusted Him to fulfill our deepest heart desire. We tried to maintain the components that make faith possible according to Hebrews 11:1. We knew we had to keep hoping for a child even though he or she wasn't in our lives yet. As much as we prayed, I still struggled with the reality of not being pregnant yet.

At that time, I didn't realize just how many emotions a woman could feel while trying to conceive. I didn't fully understand what happens during pregnancy. I had an idea but I definitely experienced some surprises along the way. I came to understood most of the emotions were caused by hormones. There were so many emotions (e.g. joy, happiness, sadness, doubt, anger, frustration). I spent a lot time reflecting on my life and all that had occurred to bring me to such an important moment.

When I was pregnant, I wanted life to just stop some days. And then – when my pregnancy was over – life did...stop.

# The Preparation

*"Every hardship; every joy;*
*every temptation is a challenge of the spirit;*
*that the human soul may prove itself.*
*The great chain of necessity wherewith we are bound has divine*
*significance; and nothing happens which has not some service*
*in working out the sublime destiny of the human soul."* - Elias A. Ford

# Chapter 1
# Past Lessons

Life can equip us without even letting us know we are in training. I didn't realize it, but my life experiences had been molding me and preparing me for this important time in my life. Mothering an angel is no small task!

**My Early Days**

As a child, I was often sick. When I was two years old, I needed a blood transfusion and was diagnosed with iron-deficiency anemia. That marked the beginning of my parents being extra careful about everything. My parents had me on multivitamins and eating liver and onions at least once a week. My mother would often check my fingertips and my eyes to make sure they were a normal pinkish color. My parents kept this up throughout my entire childhood.

As a result, I soon began to experience many social anxieties. I was always cold, so I had to dress in clothes that covered. My mother constantly made sure my hair was styled and my clothes were nice. She didn't want me to look sick – even though I was tired all the time. I was allowed to play with other children but not too much because my parents were afraid of the rough-housing. They feared I'd become scarred and bleed. I was subconscious about my appearance and worried about if I would get sick again. I played by myself often. Since I didn't want to explain why I was so cold all the time or why I needed to rest for a minute, I discovered boys made the best friends because they were less judgmental.

**Discovering God**

My parents raised me to believe God exists, and that He made the heavens and the earth but that's about all. Sometimes I went to church with my cousin who went every Sunday with her mom (my aunt). It was my grandma (my father's mother) who most often took me to church when I was little. I didn't realize it but one day I was going to appreciate the impact she made on my life.

## Not Your Typical Teenager

The summer before I started high school, I took a job with a neighborhood church organization cleaning downtown bus stops and some area landscapes with other teenagers. I was excited because my dad helped me start a savings account since I would get paid every two weeks. I was feeling more confident and ready to learn about being independent. Instead, as the summer progressed I found myself becoming extra fatigued. I was physically drained every day even though all I did was eat, sleep, and work. I knew I had iron-deficiency anemia; so, I ignored my fatigue and continued with my daily routine.

One night I couldn't sleep well because of terrible stomach pains. I went to our neighborhood clinic located right behind our house. They took blood work and told me they would call my parents if anything unusual came back.

The next day, I got up and went to work as usual. As we prepared to leave, the group leader told me to stay behind because my parents were on their way to get me. My mind raced and soon I was thinking of worst case scenarios like mama or grandma was sick.

## A Pretty Bad Scenario

When my parents pulled up, I got in the car and saw one of my duffel bags on the seat next to me. I noticed mama had been crying. My daddy then told me I had to go to the hospital to have an emergency blood transfusion. I instantly became scared. The last time I had a blood transfusion was when I was a little baby. Why would I need a blood transfusion at 14?

When I arrived at the hospital, the medical staff immediately began an IV to begin the blood transfusion. The nurse who examined me at the clinic came into my room along with the other doctors. Soon, they were asking me many questions. I found out that my iron had gotten so dangerously low that I could have died in my sleep. I learned that having proper iron levels helps to distribute oxygen throughout the body. If the level gets too low and oxygen isn't distributed, it can be fatal.

The doctors reviewed the notes from my exam and asked about the stomach pains. I told them I was still having them; and, it was hard for me to sleep in certain positions. They continued to ask their normal medical questions and soon red flags were seen by the doctors. They scheduled an endoscopy and colonoscopy for two weeks from that day. I was nervous and anxious as I awaited the additional tests. My stomach pains worsened. I couldn't sleep because of pain and fear. I wondered what could possibly be wrong.

## Faith Ignited

One night I decided to pray to God. Honestly, I didn't even know how to pray. I didn't know if God was hearing my prayers. I just remember telling God to please heal me of whatever was wrong with me. I didn't want to be afraid all the time. I had already experienced so much fear in my childhood. For me, it just didn't seem normal. I loved my job and learning independence like a typical teenager. "Please God, let everything be okay," I prayed.

## The Real Worst Case Scenario

The results of the endoscopy and colonoscopy revealed a mass in my colon. I had surgery to remove it one week later. I stayed in the hospital for several weeks to monitor the success of the surgery. Still, I was unprepared for the news the doctor came and told me.

"The mass was cancerous," he said. My official diagnosis was Non-Hodgkins Lymphoma.

When I heard the doctor say cancer, I instantly started crying. I had already lost two grandparents to cancer. The only connection to cancer I understood was death. I thought was going to die. I began to think about how much I would miss my family and friends. I thought about never getting married or being able to have children. The doctors explained the plan for chemotherapy and instead offered hope for a bright future. Based on their prognosis, I would live a long and happy life. However, they explained to me the side effects of chemotherapy. "You may lose all your hair and potentially be unable to have children when you are older."

After hearing this reality, my confidence level went so low. I feared starting high school with no hair and being on chemotherapy. I wondered how people would treat me. Would teachers understand why I'm missing class when I have chemo appointments? It seemed as if the confident and independent young lady I wanted to become was no longer within reach.

I truly believed my life was going to be cut short or drastically different because of my diagnosis. But, God had a different plan for me.

### My Testimony

Starting at birth, all events that happen in our life are connected and divinely designed to develop us into who He created us to be. I learned that life is precious because I almost lost it (more than once) before I was 14. These experiences birthed several characteristics that I learned matched what God has ordained for my life. I now know and understand that I am created in His image.[1] God possesses all strength, courage, boldness, and wisdom. He knew in order to teach me these attributes, I had to go through some life experiences. I can now declare that I have strength – I am courageous – I have spiritual boldness – and I will continuously gain wisdom!

### Personal Reflections

1.  Think back to your childhood. Remember something that was significant for you. How did it make you feel? Did you feel your childhood was normal or abnormal?

2.  Can you identify the root cause of these emotions: fear, anger, regret, bitterness, sadness, or any negative thought?

3.  When did it start? Were you a child or teenager? If so, now is a great time to start dealing with those emotions holding you back from your God-given destiny?

End Notes

1 – Genesis 1:27

# *Write It Out*

# Chapter 2
# Growing in Faith

*"Therefore I take pleasure in infirmities...in persecutions, in distresses for Christ's sake: for when I am weak, then am I strong" – 2 Corinthians 12:10 (KJV)*

Truthfully, life did change for me after my diagnosis. I was not the same. I spent the remainder of the summer in and out of the hospital; and, I vividly remember that most of my nights were spent alone. But as a result, I began to pray more. As I began to pray more, I started to understand the spiritual and natural sides of life. I remember writing a letter to my parents during that time to apologize for my behavior as a teenager. Before my diagnosis, I didn't realize life was precious.

Chemotherapy was difficult. I was grateful for the nurses who cried with me and helped me face the side effects. I just did the best I could to make it through each day. But even though I was doing chemo treatments, I still worried that I could die. They told me that even the chemicals in the chemo were lethal if administered incorrectly.

**Growing Closer with Grandma Charlotte**

It was definitely hard going on with life as usual. I started high school as a home school student because I was doing outpatient chemo treatments. Since both of my parents worked, I needed a guardian at home. My grandma, Charlotte, came over to help. I'd always considered her the greatest of grandmothers. Growing up, I spent weekends at her house. If I had no good pajamas to wear, she would just grab some left over fabric and make me a night gown on her sewing machine. She is best described as a strong, Christian woman who talked a lot about God. In fact, she was the person who first took me to church. She often told me never to play with my salvation. I didn't need it often, but -when I did- her discipline was strong but loving. By the time she finished correcting me, I totally understood how I was wrong and why I needed to shape up. My grandfather, her husband, was one of the ones who had already died of cancer by the time I was diagnosed. During my battle, I considered him an angel watching over me.

Spending one-on-one time with my grandma allowed us to become very close. I confided in my grandma how I was afraid of going back to school with no hair and how my peers might treat me. I also told her I had been praying to God about learning more about becoming a Christian. She encouraged me to start reading the Bible to gain more understanding about God. She also said to find a church to join and get involved with church ministry. She assured me that it would help me learn about living a Christian lifestyle that would please God.

Grandma and I developed a routine and made our way through each day. Even though I was always tired, I stayed ahead in my studies and did well in high school. By second semester of freshman year, the chemotherapy stopped and I was able to attend classes at the high school campus.

**Developing a Personal Relationship with God**

I was fifteen years old when I joined my family church and was baptized. I was excited about going to church every Sunday. I learned more about God and how to develop my relationship with Him. As my relationship with God grew, my confidence level began to shift. I soon understood that people really didn't know my story so whatever they said didn't bother me.

My fear about life and not having a future began to change. I learned that God was the source for my blessings; and, I didn't have to fear anyone because God would protect me. I didn't do everything right, but I learned that once you become a Christian, sanctification is still a process (just like my physical healing). It's amazing how God will work all things together for your good!

Truthfully, I believe that because I found God and got involved with church activities, God granted me favor and opened doors of opportunity to further my education. During my junior year of high school, I applied for scholarships. By the end of my junior year, I was awarded several and a full-tuition scholarship to Purdue University. My parents were so proud. I was thrilled! I knew my parents did not have a college fund for me. In our household, my parents just wanted my sister and me to at least finish high school.

I was a graduate of the class of 2000 – the group of children that many consider Generation Y or Gen Y.[1] But, I went straight to college in August of 2000 and graduated in May 2004 with a Bachelor of Science in Computer Information Technology. In November of 2004, I began working for a well-known insurance company. Ironically, it was the exact same insurance company that worked with the church organization I worked for when I was 14. (Isn't God funny that way?) I even purchased my first home in early 2005. I finally felt like my life was normal!

My relationship with God had grown. I'd joined a new ministry and attended several wonderful Christian conferences that taught me who I am in God and empowered me to use the power of prayer. My confidence level increased when I began to recognize my worth in God. I decided not to allow the opinion of others to change my perception of me. The fear and anxiety of being judged by others was no longer overtaking my life.

### My Testimony

I've had some major spiritual encounters throughout my life. These spiritual encounters were strengthening and teaching me for the coming tests that I was about to endure. God knew I had to mature in Him. I was in my late twenties and the future obstacles would test my trust in God. I wasn't leaning on my own understanding[2] anymore. It took time to learn God did not give us the spirit of fear but He has given us power, love, and a sound mind.[3]

### Personal Reflections

1. What were your spiritual encounters like? Were they always with the Christian faith? How did they change your perspective about the Christian faith?

2. What ministries are you actively participating in? Inside or outside of your church?

3. Can you give credit and thanksgiving to someone who helped you down the path to Christianity? Have you identified your angel?

## Endnotes

1 – http://en.wikipedia.org/wiki/Millennials

2 – Proverbs 3:5

3 – 2 Timothy 1:7

# *Write It Out*

# Chapter 3
# Nothing is Impossible with God

2005 was a big year! It was in September 2005 that I met my future husband, Iradel. During our courtship, he met grandma Charlotte. By that time, she was diagnosed with stomach cancer and had been in a nursing home for a few years. Grandma Charlotte was very pleased with Iradel and knew instinctively that he was going to take good care of me. On September 17, 2008, my grandmother passed away. Three days later, Iradel and I were married on September 20, 2008. People thought I was going to be an emotional mess for the wedding. But, I talked to God a lot during that time. When I prayed, God assured me my grandma was there at the wedding in spirit.

Grandma Charlotte became an angel for me and my husband. In life, she helped lead me down the path of finding God for myself. It was her instructions and demonstrations that taught me how to follow God. Grandma Charlotte taught me to follow and lean on God to become the confident woman I wanted to be. She helped me start the healing process of overcoming past fears, doubts, and anxieties.

**Walking by Faith**

As much as I had learned about God and the confidence I had in Him, the obstacle of trying to start a family awakened negative thoughts. As happy as I was to be Iradel's wife, marriage was a spiritual test for me because I had to finally open a secret wound – not knowing if I could conceive. Like most couples, we talked a lot about starting a family during our courtship. Our discussions even included adoption. My husband knew about my past history of cancer and the possibility that I could be unable to conceive. When I explained to him what the doctors said about the side effects of chemotherapy, he simply told me we would both pray about it and see what God says. I was the one who had to get past all of my doubts and fears.

The emotions and thoughts that soon came back to me were all too familiar. I loved children! I thought babies were the most precious little people ever! Whenever I played with babies in church, I would secretly think to myself, "I hope I can have a baby someday." I soon began to fear how my husband would feel about me if I didn't bear him a child. Would he still be attracted to me? Would I still be considered a good wife? Would I be considered a Christian wife? I feared he would judge me, even though he said he wouldn't and hadn't.

## Patience in the Meantime

The process of trying to conceive just added to my fears and anxieties. Months and years went by. Test after test came back negative. The negative results caused more negative thoughts to come to my mind. My husband remained so loving and non-judgmental during the whole process. He soon began to have thoughts about himself. What if he was the problem and not me? I offered him the same love and absence of judgment he'd shown toward me.

Eventually, I did blood work and ended up at a fertility specialist. Some of the tests were not bad but some were painful. The physical obstacles were beginning to match the emotional ones. However, the tests came back and indicated no issues were found. Finally, this was a positive outcome for me and my husband.

The fertility specialist still wanted me to take some fertility medications since conception didn't happen within the one year time frame. At first, I was a little afraid of the side effects of hormone medications. I was already emotional and didn't want to be any worse. I didn't want to become intolerable for my husband. We also had to pray about the final costs of such a process! When we discovered the cost and limits of our insurance coverage, we researched adoption to compare overall costs. Both were extremely expensive. I was finding it harder and harder not to doubt if I was supposed to have child.

There seemed to be so many road blocks and obstacles! I thought about my past medical history, the limited insurance coverage of fertility medications, and the fact that we did not have a lot of money to pay initial upfront costs for adoption. I tried my very best not to take my emotions out on my husband. I was frustrated, fearful, sad, and emotionally drained.

Still, we continued to pray.

We found ourselves surrounded by people who were also praying for us. We didn't realize this at first. However, soon we had many people just encouraging us to believe in God and to trust Him. They didn't know our situation because we didn't tell them. It was like God was using different people who genuinely cared for us to pass along the message that He's been listening to our prayers. It was God's way of giving our hands a little 'squeeze' to remind us that He is still in control.

After one round of taking specialty medications, we tested positive on a home pregnancy test! It seemed unreal; and, it took an eternity to arrive! We were so excited and happy. We told our close friends and relatives. I really didn't know how to feel besides happy and excited. I wasn't nervous at that point because to me God just performed a miracle in our lives!

### My Testimony

For nothing is impossible with God![1] Let me make absolutely sure the devil knows just how severely he was defeated. I had cancer when I was 14. I endured chemotherapy that was so strong it was supposed to cause sterilization of my reproduction organs. The cancer I had was supposed come back in 5 to 7 years. The doctors told me if I wanted the chance to have children I should try before I was 25 years old. HOWEVER … I was 30 years old, cancer free since that first diagnosis and treatment. ALL the tests showed no sterilization of my reproductive organs, and I was pregnant! You can't tell me my God isn't a healer![2]

### Personal Reflections

1. What strongholds are causing you to doubt the impossible?

2. Can you identify the reasons (i.e. finances, repeated obstacles, etc.)?

3. What have you been praying about secretly? Can you identify how God has been 'squeezing' your hand?

4. Can you identify those prayers that have been answered in your life or someone else's? How did it make you feel?

End Notes

1 – Mark 10:27

2 – 1 Peter 2:24, Isaiah 53:5, Psalm 103:3

# *Write It Out*

# The Process

*"There are two ways to live your life.*
*One is as though nothing is a miracle.*
*The other is as though everything is a miracle"* - *Albert Einstein*

# Chapter 4
# I'm Pregnant!

### 1st Trimester – The Joyfulness

After the first ultrasound, we were filled with so much joy! We felt undecided if we wanted to tell people right away or wait for three months. Many people like to wait until after the three month mark during the second trimester when the risks of miscarriage or complications have lessened. We told our best friends first who were jubilant for us. By the middle of January 2013, everyone knew, including our family.

I had to mentally remind myself, "I'm pregnant." The one thing I thought was impossible was now manifested. I knew there was a God, and He was real! As I continued with my first sets of maternity care ultrasounds, we watched the miracle unfold. I saw the little 'alien' in my womb develop, and I was just awe struck. I've known where babies come from since kindergarten. I was taught that when two people who love each other come together, they produce life. As I grew up, I was always the one in the audience who watched the miracle of life take place in other people lives. Now, I was on stage and everyone else was watching as the miracle took place in my life!

The hospital we selected, Community North Hospital, was one of the top providers in our city. They had a wonderful maternity ward, and the staff exemplified the true meaning of family development. The nurses were so wonderful. During the first trimester, I tried to make doctor appointments in the morning so my husband could come despite his work schedule but there were a few he couldn't attend. One particular visit, the nurse and I could see the heart beating during the ultrasound. It was so amazing! The nurse said, "I love to see those little hearts." She said our baby's heart was the most beautiful she had seen in a while. It was strong and you could see those developing valves were working and pumping life through the tiny, little body. I remember thinking I could listen to sound of that heart beat all day long!

As I began to show, our church family and regular family grew seemingly more excited than we were. The church mothers were trying to predict the sex of the baby based on my symptoms. It was hard for them because

I really didn't have 'bad' symptoms. I didn't have morning sickness but I was tired. My only cravings included pizza and chocolate milk. I could eat pizza every day (and I did for a couple of weeks). I also craved fruit – mainly pineapple.

Whenever people would ask us if we wanted a boy or a girl, we simply replied 'a strong and healthy baby'. People didn't believe us when we said that but many people didn't know our whole story. Although this may not seem like much, we didn't want to limit God's blessing. We knew no matter if it was a boy or a girl, our child was a blessing.

We tried not to think of negative facts related to pregnancy. For example, the risk of miscarriage is higher in the first trimester. Among women who know they are pregnant, about 10%-15% end in miscarriage.[1] By the second trimester, that percentage goes down to 1%-5% but there is also the possibility of stillbirth.

I remember having dreams about discovering the baby not moving or as I was giving birth the baby didn't cry. I just blew them off – 'I rebuke you Satan' is what I remember saying. It is said that 1 in 160 pregnancies, stillbirth occurs.[2] My husband and I both knew of people, family and friends, who had experienced a pregnancy loss. We understood the process of pregnancy is difficult. Women make it look easy but the level of emotions, hormones, and physical changes that one experience is not always pleasant.

Most women have heard the biblical story of Adam and Eve. The lesson it provides is about the fall of man and sin entering into the world. In Genesis, God commanded that Adam and Eve not eat the fruit off a certain tree. Eve was enticed by a serpent (Satan) to taste anyway and she then persuaded Adam to do the same. The curse that God gave women for the disobedience Eve committed includes the pain of childbearing and labor.[3] This curse is one that cannot be broken. This curse came from God, not Satan – so this meant serious punishment for disobedience. Fortunately, curses from Satan can be broken because he is a liar[4] and deceiver. Satan wants to keep strongholds on you so you can't reach what God has promised you but you are more than a conqueror![5] God is truth and righteous – He breaks and defeats all that Satan tries to do to His children.

I believe the curse related to childbearing was His reminder to us that when God commands obedience, He means it. During my pregnancy, I was obedient and as faithful as possible! While I typically strive to be faithful to God, I was extra diligent because He allowed (blessed) me to even become pregnant. I wanted to make sure to give Him all the praise, honor, and glory! I knew I didn't get pregnant all by myself so the credit couldn't go to me or my husband. The credit belonged to God.

The miracle and process of life is one that is truly astonishing. The fact that God allowed such small specimens to come together inside my uterus and develop into a human being is amazing! God is an awesome God! I felt so much joy each time I went to prenatal visits because each time it was like my biggest dream came true! I was pregnant! The evidence of the promise became more and more real each time they did blood work and ultrasounds. Each day, as we yet live, it should be enough evidence to know that His promises are manifesting in our lives! Isn't God a great and awesome God? I think so! I believe so! I know so!

### 2nd Trimester – The Gladness

As the second trimester began, we were excited because we finally found out the gender of the baby.  Unfortunately, my husband couldn't make that appointment but I was texting him 'play by play' notes. As the ultrasound began, our little one was moving but not really paying much attention to the lady trying to look for 'the little m' or 'the little turtle' (I promise I'm not making this up – just the verbiage used by the nurses). Eventually, the little person moved to sit directly on top of the ultrasound monitoring wand. We were having a girl (no 'little turtle' – the 'little m' appeared)! I told my husband; and, we were so thrilled. The joy was just overwhelming. We had already picked out a name if it was a girl – Charlotte Evelina Price. Charlotte was my grandmother who died three days before our wedding and Evelina was my husband's mother who I consider the greatest mother-in-law of all time. Both represented a spiritual strength rare to find nowadays. We wanted our little girl to carry on the legacy of that spiritual strength and her name to represent her being a child of God. Her life didn't belong to us. God privileged us to be stewards over her soul to help direct it back to Him.

We knew and understood what God had commanded and demanded of us. When God charged Adam and Eve to be fruitful and multiply[6], it just didn't mean go out and have lots of children. Some of the synonyms for fruitful are productive, profitable, rewarding, successful, rich, and prolific. We understood that with the new calling of parenthood, no matter what, this child had to be taught and guided to become a productive resource for the Kingdom of God. God placed that charge on us to help with this process of development for this soul. The two commands, fruitful and multiply, go together for a reason. When we are fruitful, multiplication takes place. When we strive to live a life that is rewarding and profitable, it's our God-given duty to ensure that we bless others. We must multiply the Kingdom of God – increase the Kingdom of God with more true Christian believers. When we help to increase the Kingdom of God, this brings greater glory to God. We then get to see more glorious manifestations of how God takes care of His people. This is how we are to be fruitful and multiply.

Baby Charlotte soon became popular with all the nurses, friends, and family. She wasn't 'camera shy' whenever we had an ultrasound done. She would face the camera often. However, she would fall asleep if she felt the ultrasound was taking too long. As she continued to develop, I figured out that pineapple made her happy. I can only assume it was because of the sweetness of the fruit juices. Her movements became stronger as the weeks progressed and the reality of pregnancy kicked in real good! My body truly made the major physical changes (e.g. growing belly, breasts, and skin complexion changes). I was officially a pregnant lady!

I had no doubt this beautiful little girl would bring such joy and gladness to our lives. The thought of motherhood was a little scary. God reassured me that if I listened to Him, I would be a good mother. As a mother, you want the best for your child. You want your child to do better than you. It was like when Jesus told his disciples they are to do greater works.[7] We expected that Charlotte would have questions and because God made us in His image where we have freedom of choice, she would choose whether to follow God or not. I planned on being very honest with Charlotte about life and how this world has some major evil spirits lurking about. I also planned to tell her that because life is all about decisions and choices, we must strive to make the right ones. Right choices align with God's Will more easily than the wrong ones. I planned to explain to her how she would know she'd made a right choice by the peace within her heart and spirit. Then, I planned to teach her about being patient and not being anxious for anything[8] but to instead always go to God and seek after Him first and all His righteousness[9] so He could add what she needed and wanted. I also planned to tell her the choices won't come easy and that sometimes she would make the wrong choice but God is a forgiving God[10] unlike men and women. I wanted her to know you can always return to God; and, He will accept you with open arms because you are the apple of His eye![11]

The thought of motherhood and raising an amazing child gave me a level of gladness I couldn't even imagine. Soon I knew I would need to plan a baby shower and I was eagerly anticipating the third trimester to experience even greater joy and gladness!

### 3rd Trimester – The Calm before the Storm

The planning of the baby shower began in June of 2013. We registered at all the major baby stores and emphatically wanted some wonderful gifts for our baby Charlotte! I scheduled a 3D ultrasound where the pictures would capture more of a 'life-like' image of her. The 3D ultrasound nurse told me to eat 30 minutes before coming so that the baby would be awake and moving. I was approximately 33 ½ weeks when I had the 3D ultrasound done. Charlotte gave a wonderful performance! The nurse was very entertained and even said she was the most active and happiest baby she had seen a long time. She would laugh, smile, pose with the pouting lips – she was ready to make her way into this world!

My husband and I also scheduled some maternity portraits and everyone thought they were wonderful. By this time in my pregnancy, I was feeling heavy and tired. I remember my feet and ankles were often swollen. Fortunately, it was July and watermelon was in season! I was eating watermelon like it was prime rib. It really helped with the swelling and kept me well hydrated.

The theme of the baby shower was Minnie Mouse. We wanted simple but nice. She received wonderful gifts and cute clothes. Our best friends hosted the baby shower. All of our close friends and family came to celebrate Charlotte's life. Honestly, we didn't care if someone didn't bring a gift – we wanted them to come and celebrate her life. She was our first baby, and we didn't want anyone to miss out on the occasion.

After the parties and celebrations, time was drawing closer for her arrival. I stopped working during the second week of August. Charlotte's official due date was August 30th. My husband didn't want me to sit at home all day; so, we would walk around the mall sometimes. I went to prenatal visits every week to check for dilation and any cervix changes. I had experienced no changes at that point. However, that week before she was due, I experienced one change. The movement had stopped being so frequent.

I remember having a prenatal appointment in the early part of the week – the week of August 19th. All seemed fine. They even found the baby's heart beat although it took a while to find. After that appointment, however, I felt very uneasy because of the time it took for the doctor to locate the heartbeat. I thought I was probably over-reacting but soon I couldn't feel any more movement.

It was two days after a normal prenatal visit. I was at 9 months. I woke up and felt very uneasy. I couldn't feel any movement from Charlotte. I told Iradel Charlotte isn't moving like she normally does after I eat. I called the on-call nurse with a very shaky voice. I explained my condition and concern. The nurse advised me to come in for a stress test. The nurse and my husband both told me that everything was going to be ok. It was hard for me to believe them. Right before I went in for the stress test, my husband gently poked my belly and said something to Charlotte. My stomach moved as though Charlotte was responding to her daddy.

As I arrived at the doctor's office, the nurses kept reassuring me that everything was probably fine. The nurses told me that during the last part of the pregnancy there's often not enough room for the baby to move so movement isn't as frequent. I did the only thing I knew to do. I shook my head and smiled. I didn't respond with any words because I was too nervous.

The nurses connected me to the monitoring system but couldn't locate her heartbeat. They kept reassuring me and said let's have a doctor try. After several minutes, they transferred me to another room and had the doctor on staff (not my OB/GYN) use the smaller monitor. No heartbeat. By this time, my smile was gone. I was more than nervous and anxious to understand what was happening. I'd blocked out all the reassurances. I needed to know if something was wrong because there was still no heartbeat. Finally, the doctor and a nurse took me to the ultrasound room. As the nurse moved the small monitor all around my belly, the first thing I noticed was no heartbeat. The second thing I noticed was no movement on the monitor.

The silence was loud.

### My Testimony

Although I heard no heartbeat and the silence in that ultrasound room was loud, a faint voice inside of me began to speak. This faint voice was God's spirit reassuring me that Charlotte was doing ok. I didn't fully comprehend what it meant because what was in front me didn't match what the faint voice was saying. How could Charlotte be ok with no heartbeat? Later, I realized the heartbeat wasn't the source that made her live. The source that made her live was God. In Acts 17:28 it says that in Him we live and move and have our being. I realized that Charlotte lives with God (sooner than when I'd hoped) but she really is doing ok.

### Personal Reflections

1. What lies has the enemy tried to tell you?

2. Besides the miracle of life, think about the other miracles God performs daily. What miracle did He allow you to see today? Once you specify the miracle, thank Him for it!

3. How do you help multiply the Kingdom of God? If you aren't sure, take some time and see how you can help.

4. What has God made you the steward over? (Is it children? Are you the manager at your job? Are you responsible for a large group of people?)

5. How are you becoming a better steward?

6. Consider all the excuses that you keep you from doing more for Him. I encourage you to reflect on what is separating you from God.

End Notes

1 – http://www.marchofdimes.org/loss/miscarriage.aspx

2 – http://www.marchofdimes.org/loss/stillbirth.aspx

3 – Genesis 3:16

4 – John 8:44

5 – Romans 8:37

6 – Genesis 1:28

7 – John 14:12

8 – Philippians 4:6

9 – Matthew 6:33

10 – 1 John 1:9

11 – Deuteronomy 32:10; Psalm 17:8

# *Write It Out*

# Chapter 5
# Shock & Numbness

I tried to muster up a smile and look at the doctor and nurse who by this time were whispering to each other. The doctor slowly walked around to my left side and grabbed my hand. He looked me in the eyes and said, "I'm sorry but we can't find the heartbeat…" By this time, I wasn't smiling at all. I'm not sure what expression was on my face but I suddenly felt a coldness flush over my body.

He looked me in the eyes and uttered the words that I thought were a completely cruel joke. He told me that Charlotte was no longer alive. It took a moment before I could comprehend what he said. I knew when I finally understood what he said because I began to cry hysterically. My hands covered my face in sheer embarrassment and disgust.

**The Nightmare Came True**

Honestly, I thought I was having that bad dream again, and I just needed to wake myself up. Then, I told them to please check again, and they did. Silence and stillness. That's when I just went numb. The doctor slowly asked me if I had anyone I needed to call and through the tears I answered with my husband's name.

As I called my husband, my hand was shaking so badly. I don't even recall how the cell phone got in my hand but it did. I dialed my husband's number and the instant he answered the phone, I cried. I'm not sure if my words were even audible but he understood. I told him he needed to come to the hospital. He tried to ask me what was wrong but I just remember saying please come to the hospital. He cried and said, "Ok, ok, Baby – I'm on my way." The doctor and nurse guided me off the exam table and led me to another exam room so I could wait for my husband.

When my husband arrived, I was in a room wishing I was in a nightmare from which I would soon wake up. My husband fell to his knees in front of me and hugged me so tight. We both just cried. After several minutes, he got up and we both just sat there. Nurses came in and hugged me while crying as well. Once our official doctor arrived, we really didn't know what to expect next.

## The Birthing Experience

After conversing with our doctor, we made a plan to induce my labor. As my wheelchair traveled down the halls, it seemed surreal. As I arrived to my maternity suite, I was just numb from head to toe. As I went through all the routine procedures of prep and dressing, the thought of Charlotte not being alive was just incomprehensible.

Friends, family, and church family came to visit us while waiting for the arrival of Charlotte. My husband and I just kept smiling. Then, when everyone would leave, we would cry. I had requested to not feel as much physical pain as possible because the emotional pain was enough. I slept during the majority of my labor. Eventually, I was ready to push and the pain of being fully dilated awakened a type of anger in me that made me want to run and hide.

I closed my eyes a lot while I pushed Charlotte out. I kept wishing I could just wake up. I kept thinking maybe she will come out crying after all. In less than 10 minutes, Charlotte arrived! She was 6 pounds, 14 ounces, and 21 inches long. Once she arrived, it was quiet. The stillness in the room was almost like in a motion picture film. It was just her shell. No life or spirit. Her spirit was already back with God.

The nursing staff cleaned her body and prepped it like a normal newborn. I appreciated the fact that they treated her as if she was still alive. I could only imagine what other hospitals may do but I was thankful that this hospital treated Charlotte's body with love, care, and respect. It gave me so much comfort.

She was so beautiful – she had a head full of black hair and chunky cheeks. We allowed the nurses to dress her to take pictures. As soon as she was dressed and wrapped, my husband held her wrapped body in the baby blanket and started to pray. As a licensed minister, he anointed her with oil and prayed over her – dedicating her back to God. It was a sad but thankful occasion. My husband and I were comfortable telling God thank you but we didn't know how we were doing it.

It was so quiet in the room although the nurses and doctors were still cleaning me up and doing their normal routine. Finally, I held her. She was so beautiful. The cheeks, the hair, the smooth skin – our baby was better than everyone else's (so we thought like every other parent does)! However, even while holding her, we didn't feel what most new parents felt. The nurses didn't talk to us about how to change her diaper or how to give her first bath. Their conversation to us was about how to make funeral arrangements and who to contact concerning the special stipend to help with funeral costs. As numb as I was, I somehow kept smiling and just letting everyone know I'd be fine. But I really didn't know if I would be fine – especially once we left the hospital.

The book of Ecclesiastes is often considered the answer to the famous question – What is the meaning of life? Solomon is considered the author of this book. He speaks about working hard and enjoying life which is what God wants us to do. I remember working on my Master's in Business Administration during my pregnancy. We completed a study of Ecclesiastes. I reflected on chapter 3 while in the hospital because it focused on seasons of life. Sometimes, it's tempting to narrow down the seasons of life to the same framework as weather seasons. However, life isn't that simple. In Ecclesiastes chapter 3, multiple seasons are discussed for the various seasons of life. On August 23rd, the stillbirth of Charlotte was our season of weeping, mourning, loss, hate, keeping silent – it was our season to be human.

While I was in the hospital, I felt protected. I only had to focus on myself, my husband, and Charlotte's body. I did the normal tasks of showering and eating. The initial shock and numbness started to fade after a few days went by. I would still smile when family and friends would visit us. It was my way of masking the pain and faking my real emotions.

The conversations I had with God while in the hospital were brief. I wasn't sure what to say because my heart couldn't grasp the 'why' of this experience. When the day came for me to leave the hospital, I didn't know what emotions were coming my way. As I kissed Charlotte goodbye and made my way down to the car, it seemed the motion picture movie started again.

I watched as other new mothers carried car seats while I just had a bag of dirty clothes. Their smiles were so proud and happy. I had no smile. Not this time. I couldn't fake it this time. I didn't want to fake how I really felt any longer. I'd just lost my very first baby. I couldn't smile about that. I didn't have any feelings of pride or happiness. As I watched those new mothers, I started to feel ashamed, embarrassed, and like an outsider. I didn't have anything in common with these women. This wasn't the normal moment that I'd hoped for.

## My Testimony

Although we are made in God's image[1] we still are born into a world where the flesh still operates. That means we have emotions that can overwhelm us. To even begin with any emotional healing process, you must acknowledge the brokenness that is present. We couldn't give room to the devil[2] so we acknowledged the various emotions caused by the stillbirth of our first born. It affected every area of our lives – spiritual strength, marriage, self-esteem, faith, etc. Once it was time to leave the hospital, we had to accept that we wanted to heal from this hurt and pain. The only way that would happen – God would have to do it. Not our parents, pastor, friends, or loved ones. Only God would give us the healing we needed to make us whole again.[3]

## Personal Reflections

1. What major life event(s) caused you to feel deep emotional pain? What were your initial feelings and/or reactions?

2. What were you conversations like with God when something devastating happened in your life?

3. What do you do to hide your true emotions? (i.e. smile? laugh? tell jokes?)

End Notes

1 – Genesis 1:27

2 – Ephesians 4:27

3 – Matthew 9:22

## _Write It Out_

_(lined writing space)_

# Chapter 6
# Sadness & Fear

Being back at home was hard. The first couple of weeks were extremely exhausting because we had to arrange the funeral and still manage to respond to all the condolences that we received. We appreciated the phones calls, text messages, and gifts. It sort of helped but I mostly wanted to hide so I didn't have to deal with it all.

Once the funeral was over, I did isolate myself. I took time off from work and just stayed home. I didn't feel like going out or talking much. My husband and I ended up buying a puppy. Some thought we did this to help with the coping and healing process. However, this puppy didn't help with that at all. I still had to heal physically from the pregnancy; and, I didn't want to make any emotional connection with anyone – that included an animal.

**The Healing Begins**

I had difficulty sleeping for a few weeks. I felt sadness and fear because as I began to physically heal and go out, I didn't know how to address those who either knew or didn't know about Charlotte. Most of my co-workers knew so they were very polite and didn't ask me any questions. My family members who knew were very gentle as they would call and approach me to give me a hug. However, I did have to encounter some who didn't know. I'm not sure if it was harder for them or me when I told them. I didn't want to make anybody else sad because I was sad. There were various reactions from the people who didn't know. Some just hugged me instantly. Some just said they were sorry. Some couldn't say anything.

My emotions were definitely causing me to be very anti-social. After seeing people's response and people trying to 'walk on eggshells' around me, I just wanted to stop interacting with people all together. They didn't know how to handle me; and, I didn't know how to handle them. I wasn't upset with them or afraid of the people. It was their reactions. When I had to tell people that Charlotte was stillborn, it was like I was that doctor who had to tell me that Charlotte was not alive anymore. Telling that type of news over and over wasn't something I looked forward to doing.

I was sad because I wasn't the mother I thought I was going to be or should be. When I would look at Charlotte's bassinet, crib, changing table, clothes, diapers, bottles, baby bags – it just didn't seem fair. It just didn't seem right. Something was missing and all I could think about was how alive she was inside of me but she wasn't alive outside of me.

I started to ask what I did wrong. Should I have been more adamant about getting a stress test? Should I have been more attentive to the movements and really counting them? Did I take enough dietary supplements? Did I do too much walking? Did I do too much lying down or sitting? What did I do wrong?

Then my fear really made me have terrible thoughts about who I was. My self-confidence as a wife and woman were at an all-time low. I had to ask God was this my punishment for my past sins? I knew I hadn't been perfect. I've struggled with various issues like everyone else. Was I being punished? Did I not pray enough? Did I not fast enough? Should I have given God more praise and worship? This was my conversation with God for a long time. I was so ashamed and depressed that I just figured God didn't want me to come to Him any longer.

I was even fearful of my husband and what he thought of me. I couldn't talk with my husband because I felt like I'd disappointed him. I let him down because our baby died. I was supposed to be the mother – the physical caregiver of the child for 9 months. I was supposed to know how to take care of myself and the baby. She was attached to me and - whatever happened to her- I should have known instantly that something was wrong. I thought I wasn't a good wife because if I couldn't take care of the baby inside of me, I probably couldn't take care of my husband either.

The feelings of inadequacy loomed over me as I tried to make the best of my days. I went to work and sometimes cried at my desk. When my husband would call me on my lunch break, I'd cry some more. I couldn't multi-task because I was so easily overwhelmed. My mind and my heart were so overwhelmed with emotions about Charlotte, myself, and my husband – I wasn't sure if I was going to get through it.

## My Testimony

The scripture talks about how God has not given us the spirit of fear.[1] It seemed that fear has been the root cause of many issues that I had experienced. It was fear that caused my parents to take me to the hospital when I was a child to discover I had iron-deficiency anemia. It was fear that caused me to go to the doctors when I was a teenager to finally discover I had cancer. Then it was fear that caused me to go to the doctors while 9 months pregnant to discover that my first child had died inside of me. Fear seems to cause a reaction. It caused me to run to the doctors. It also caused me to run to God who is really considered the Great Physician. In Matthew 9, Jesus teaches on who really needs God. It's not the righteous or 'the healthy' but it's the sinners or 'the sick'.[2] When I had to deal with all those emotional strongholds, I knew I was spiritually sick. I ran to God even while I was sick. I didn't wait until I stopped crying or feeling down. I went to God even when I couldn't find a true praise or worship in my heart or mind. I still found love and respect for God in small places. This was a sign that let me know that I also could achieve soundness of mind.

### Personal Reflections

1.  What are you afraid of? Do you know when your spirit of fear started?

2.  How do you recognize the need for help? When do you recognize the need for help?

3.  How do you feel when it seems like you failed? How has God allowed you to continue on after the disappointment?

End Notes

1 – 2 Timothy 1:7

2 – Matthew 9: 1-13

## _Write It Out_

# Chapter 7
# Anger & Frustration

**The Healing Continues**

Eventually, I was better able to deal with people and respond to their questions. It still wasn't easy but I knew I couldn't hide from society. I had to try and live my life as normally as I could. However, as I tried to live my life, anger and frustration began to grow in my heart.

I became angry because I had to watch other families live with their small children. As I walked in the mall, I'd see people with strollers or carrying their little babies. I would ask why I couldn't have that chance to do that. Why couldn't I carry my baby around the mall, smiling and laughing as everyone would stop and compliment her beauty? I was mad at their happiness because I couldn't have it. I didn't have it.

My anger soon became evident to my husband because I didn't know how to respond to him. Even though I knew he was dealing with his own emotions, I soon was angry with him because at times I felt like he should just want to hold me or console me. I didn't understand how men dealt with their emotions – especially when something like this happens. I just expected my husband to know that I needed to be held at any time. When he wouldn't hold me or go into his office and close the door, it made me mad. I didn't realize that was his time to cry and deal with all that he was dealing with. I thought we had to cry together all time and be near each other all the time. I soon felt alone and thought my husband just didn't understand me anymore.

My parents never made plans to come to the hospital when I was going to deliver Charlotte. They had intended to come to the house after a few weeks to visit with her. My parents were older and didn't have reliable transportation. When my parents couldn't come to the hospital when Charlotte was stillborn, I was angry with them. I felt like they weren't there at that very moment when my heart was crushed. My parents had always been there when my heart was crushed. When I was sick and couldn't play outside like the other children, my parents were there. When I was a teenager and started dating, my parents were there when I was disappointed. I was angry because I felt like they didn't put me first for the first time. I am the baby of the family; and, this was my first child. Why wouldn't my parents be there? It didn't occur to me that I had a father who was retired with only so much money to handle all the bills of the house. It truly didn't matter to me at that time. I just knew I was hurting and my parents weren't there.

In addition to all of the anger, I felt frustrated. I didn't want to deal with taking down the crib or emptying the drawers in the changing table. Charlotte's crib and changing table remained in her room for a long time. Soon I became frustrated as I would walk into her room, and she wasn't there. We had put her name on the wall and decorated the room just for her - except she was missing. It was *her* room. I was the only one allowed to go through the door that led to her room. My husband's office was off of her room but he would use the other door to get to his office.

When I tried to express my anger, fear, sadness, and frustration to my husband, it never went well. What I was trying to say didn't make any sense to him. He didn't want to tell me how he truly felt because he didn't want me to feel any more depressed. Eventually, he told me how he felt and how he was trying to deal with his emotions. Initially, I didn't understand how he could possibly feel everything I was feeling. He didn't carry Charlotte for 9 months. He didn't have to watch his diet and take vitamins every day. He didn't have to experience any of the symptoms or labor pains. He didn't have to be in that ultrasound room when there was no heartbeat to be found.

My husband tried to open up to me. However, the anger and frustration in my response caused him to shut me out. As I tried to open up to him, I was crying, screaming, and the words were jumbled. My husband stopped talking to me for few days. I didn't think he understood me; and, I couldn't understand him.

My conversations with God were no different. I soon became angry and frustrated toward God. I didn't understand His Will. It didn't make sense that God would allow me to carry Charlotte for 9 months and then not allow me to mother her here on earth. It wasn't fair that He had to take her back. I didn't understand the purpose behind the wonderful miracle that turned out be a cruel tragedy. I am a Christian and I was created in His image[1] but I never asked for my first child to die. God watched as His only son died on the cross.[2] He at least got a chance to live until he was an adult. Charlotte never made it past 9 months. I understand the scripture about not hindering the children to come to Him,[3] but why did Charlotte have to go back to Him so soon?

I was truly upset with God's Will; and, I was sure He wasn't sorry. That made it worse. I know the Bible talks about stories of Jesus weeping,[4] getting angry enough to flip over tables,[5] and even God in the Old Testament expressed anger toward His children because of disobedience and sin. However, God's Will happens no matter what - whether He feels emotions behind it or not. For me, that seemed unfair and cruel.

I didn't want to ask God for anything except my basic essentials. I was afraid to ask for anything that might mean something to me. I was even afraid to ask that He sustain my life and my husband's life. I just didn't know what His Will would involve next. I couldn't trust God like I had trusted Him before. My confidence in myself and God was not good.

### My Testimony

God has many names in the Bible. Some of these names begin with Jehovah which means God in Hebrew. Jehovah Rapha means healer.[6] Jehovah Jireh expresses He is a provider.[7] He is also called Jehovah Shalom, a God of peace.[8] I really didn't know what to call someone who I had a hard time trusting. I had anger, frustration, sadness, depression, fear, anxiety, and low self-esteem – what name was I supposed to call to get help for all those emotions? I ended up calling Him God because I needed Him for everything – peace, healing, sanctification, guidance, provision, protection, etc. I knew I had to start somewhere so God was just...God. I didn't try to make Him more pertinent in one area over another area in my life. I needed Him in every area of life to begin to truly overcome my strongholds.

### Personal Reflections

1. How do you handle the people who don't know your situation?

2. How do you handle your family and friends when they couldn't be there for you?

3. How do you react when God's Will disappoints and/or hurts you?

End Notes

1 – Genesis 1:27

2 – John 3:16

3 – Matthew 19:14

4 – John 11:30-35

5 – Matthew 21:12

6 – Jeremiah 30:17, Jeremiah 3:22, Isaiah 30:26, Isaiah 61:1, Psalm 103:3, Exodus 15:26

7 – Genesis 22:14

8 – Judges 6:24

# *Write It Out*

# The Recovery

*"Learn to get in touch with the silence within yourself and know that everything in this life has a purpose. There are no mistakes, no coincidences. All events are blessings given to us to learn from."* - *Elizabeth Kübler-Ross*

# Chapter 8
# Can I Ever Trust Him Again?

By the time I got back into the groove of things, I was still masking my true feelings. After a while, I wasn't being open with my husband anymore. We had basic conversations about eating and going to church but we didn't communicate emotionally, spiritually, or physically in any way. I felt alone and every emotion had such a strong enough grip on me that I was not doing well. It was hard to concentrate at work. I would cry at the drop of a dime. I was having anxiety attacks often. Simply put, I was overwhelmed.

I remember saying 'thank you, God' often but it never went beyond that. I never went into detail because I honestly didn't know what I was thanking Him for. It became a routine and nothing more. I felt no real confidence in God because He had lost my trust when he took my daughter. I knew God to be great and mighty because He created the heavens and the earth.[1] I just didn't think He could be trusted with my deepest desires.

I desired to be a mother, a good wife, a strong Christian woman, and a great leader. However, I felt God really didn't care about me achieving those things because I had factored in the one component that would help me to achieve those things: Charlotte Evelina Price. I had made plans to be this wonderful example for my daughter. Now, it just seemed pointless to desire such things.

**The Healing Process**

As I slowly tried to calmly talk to God, I asked Him when the pain would go away. I needed to know when I would feel like I am a real woman and a wife. How do I begin to heal? I wondered how I would ever trust God again with my heart's desires. I tried to locate books and spiritual counselors but those were overwhelming. I didn't want to deal with reading through a lot of psychological theories about dealing with grief. I also didn't want to deal with probing questions from a counselor that I was already able to answer myself.

To trust God again, I felt like He had to earn it. It seemed unfamiliar and uncomfortable for me to even think that way because God had already proven in the past that He was God. However, my trust issue wasn't with the fact that He was God. My trust issue was, "if I pray for something will His Will cause me further disappointment and hurt?" Faith is the substance of things hoped for and the evidence of things not seen.[2] My hope was to have a healthy, strong, beautiful daughter. My evidence was my pregnancy because I still wasn't seeing her physical body. My faith had all the components to help my belief. When I prayed for a child, even as I was carrying her, I believed I would receive.[3] I followed the Biblical formula. Why wasn't it as easy as 2+2=4?

I felt my trust in God was lost because I thought I had followed what His Word says to do. It was as though God failed – but He never fails. I had to begin asking myself why He never fails. I had to reflect and read about God being triumphant in my life and others. It was hard because as I kept comparing stories to my current story, it just wasn't helping me recover my trust in God again. I felt there was no comparison.

I was growing tired of being frustrated, depressed, fearful, angry, sad, and lonely. These strongholds made me even angrier with my current life because I never intended to have these kinds of strongholds happen – with or without Charlotte Evelina being physically present. I started to desire the life I had before I was pregnant with Charlotte Evelina. However, that didn't make me feel any better because then I would have missed out on all her ultrasound pictures, hearing her heartbeat, and seeing that big smile she gave us in the 3D ultrasound picture. I would have missed out on her life. It was only for 9 months but she lived.

I then decided that I wanted to feel what I felt before and while I was pregnant. The joy, spirit of expectancy, peace, happiness, contentment, eagerness, love – I wanted to be whole again. This made me think of two stories in the Bible.

The first story I thought about was about Hannah.[4] I thought about Hannah because I was able to relate to her desire for a child. She prayed with her heart and secretly where no one could hear her. I was able to relate because as I began to pray about my desire for a child, I didn't tell many people. While at church, my prayers were often silent tears of faith, trust, and desire – like Hannah. She promised God that if she did conceive, she would dedicate the child back to Him. Once I conceived and Charlotte's body was born, we dedicated her back to God.

Hannah's deep desire for a child had filled her with great anguish and grief. She had been disappointed for so many years watching other women have children. How did she manage to keep trusting God? She was even taunted for not being able to conceive. This made her think even less of herself. I was able to understand that because I was grieving and suffering with a desire for a child that I once had. I know women didn't taunt me (and probably never did) but watching other women with their newborns made me feel like I was not a real woman and my negative thoughts taunted me. Hannah trusted God. If she could do it, why couldn't I?

The second story I thought about was the woman with the issue of blood.[5] A woman with such a private issue. She went seeking treatment from so many physicians who left her sicker and broken in all areas of her life. I related to this because when we first discovered Charlotte Evelina had died, I didn't want to tell anyone. I didn't even want family to know. My baby died inside of me. How did I let that happen? When she was born, I didn't want to share the pictures we took with our phones or the pictures that the hospital kindly took with her going-home outfits. This was a private issue for me. Though unintentional, every physician that was involved in her birth left me sick and broken in all areas of my life.

The woman with the issue of blood knew about Jesus Christ because she heard about him from other people. She heard he was traveling her way and decided she needed to touch some portion of him. She'd heard about him healing other people. She didn't really know if she would be healed or not. She couldn't afford anything else. Why not trust Jesus Christ - the Son of God. She touched just the edge of His garment. It is quite possible she didn't want to alert the people of her private issue. She didn't want to make a scene, so she quickly touched what she could while He passed through. She didn't want any attention but her faith caused Jesus Christ to react. He told her because of her faith, her trust in God, she was made whole. If her faith and trust caused her to instantly recover from all her issues, why couldn't my faith and trust help me regain wholeness again?

### My Testimony

It was difficult to find encouragement in the Bible. I felt my issue was so unique. It felt like no Bible story could possibly compare with what I was feeling. However, I continued to read the story of Hannah and the woman with the issue of blood. I found that these women were dealing with emotional issues when they cried out or reached out for God. The one common denominator they both had was trust. They trusted God. I wanted to trust God again too. Their stories helped me to recognize some principles behind trusting God. The one principle that stood out the most was no matter what happens, God can restore.

### *Personal Reflections*

1.   How has life situations tested your trust in God?

2.   What Biblical struggles can you relate to? How has these encouraged you?

3.   Can you trust God with your all?

End Notes

1 – Genesis 1:1

2 – Hebrews 11:1

3 – Matthew 21:22

4 – 1 Samuel 1

5 – Luke 8:43-48

## *Write It Out*

# Chapter 9
# Can I endure the battle?

**The Fight to Overcome**

One day during a phone conversation with my husband at work, he just told me off – in a good way. Although I cried the entire time he was talking, he finally just opened up about how he was feeling and how I needed to pray again. He told me I just needed to get back into the face of God and deal with everything I had going on in my mind. I didn't tell my husband thank you because the spiritual battle was on. As my husband was talking, so was Satan.

"How dare he talk to you like this…"

"See, he doesn't love you…"

"Doesn't he know you're depressed? Why is he trying to talk about this God stuff…"

"Doesn't he know you lost a baby…"

"Doesn't he know that you are stupid…"

"You didn't even know whose heartbeat that was…"

"You could have saved your baby's life if you weren't so stupid…"

"How much of a real woman are you, anyway…"

"You aren't fit to be a mother…"

"If God was such a powerful God, why didn't He make the baby miraculously come back to life…"

After that phone conversation, I had to collect myself because I was still at work. I got through the rest of the day but the next few days I talked to myself a lot. I have always talked to myself and people often say that's a sign you have mental health issues. However, I realized I needed to talk to myself and answer myself because I had to fight for my own peace of mind and regain my trust in God again.

## The Private Deliverance Service

Finally, one night, my husband worked late (as he normally does). I decided I needed to lay prostrate before God and pour out everything my heart was feeling. I went into our bedroom and got a bed sheet. I got the oil we had anointed and poured some in my hands. I rubbed my hands together then touched my head and my heart. I laid face down on the ground. I remember starting with 'Thank you, God.' I repeated that phrase over and over again. As much as I had been talking to myself in the past several months, I really didn't know how to be honest with God about being upset with His Will. Suddenly, the atmosphere shifted and for the next hour, I cried. I cried so hard and loud, I lost my voice. God was helping to purge myself of the negative thoughts and mindset. He was leading me to wholeness again.

Eventually, I was talking to God and He was talking to me. He told me He knew I was hurt by what He had to do. He knew it was almost like He was slack concerning His promise. He said He was sorry for the pain it caused but He wasn't sorry for His Will. He reminded me about purpose and Charlotte Evelina's purpose.[1] He said even in the womb she blessed people. Then once she was back in heaven, her ministry still was effective because friends and family found peace. Charlotte Evelina's example of life caused more of her family to join the Kingdom of God. God let me know that I did nothing wrong. In fact, I did all He instructed me to do. I prayed over her, I surrounded her with Godly spirits, and I took extra care of myself to make sure she was well taken care of. God reassured me He didn't mean to hurt me, He just meant to fulfill Charlotte Evelina's purpose.

Charlotte Evelina was pure – she knew no evil. Newborns and small children are called back to heaven because their earthly assignment is complete. These little angels are special spirits who never had to face the decision of good or evil. They didn't carry the burden of growing up in a sinful world. Charlotte Evelina, like other stillborn and little children, is a special spirit specifically selected by God to serve and worship Him in heaven.

As God continued to minister to me throughout that night, I slowly believed I could trust Him again. I was ready to walk out my healing process. I was able to sleep peacefully that night. The next several days I continued to converse with God. I told my husband about what I did and all that God told me. Soon my husband and I were talking more. I could finally go into the nursery without so many emotions. The first few times I cried. But soon the tears of hurt turned into tears of praise. I was thanking God for Charlotte Evelina and all she had done for our lives. She truly was a blessing!

### My Testimony

The battle in my mind was so tough. I studied the scripture Philippians 4:6-8. I had to shift my thoughts into positive affirmation of life. I had to consider the life that Charlotte Evelina had was perfect. Not to have to worry about her growing up in this world, facing all types of demonic forces, actually brought me peace. I know I would have done everything to try and protect her. I felt I would have done a great job teaching, leading, and guiding her on how to live in this world. However, I realized that God is the best babysitter, protector, and provider for Charlotte Evelina. She is being taken care of by the best. I feel we would have been great parents but God is extraordinary.

### Personal Reflections

1. Have you had to have a real talk with yourself? How did the conversation go?

2. What has God told you about your situation?

3. How do you shift your thoughts to positive affirmation?

End Notes

1 – Romans 8:28

# _Write It Out_

# Chapter 10
## Yes - I am Victorious!

As 2014 began, I felt more positive about myself. The spirit of depression affecting the atmosphere of our home was lessening and the spirit of expectancy was taking over. We started moving forward with life. We began to seek God for some particular requests and trust Him to answer. We understood that the process of trusting God is not meant to be easy. We felt comfortable enough to seek Him for the answer and trusted that He would guide us.

My birthday, March 31st, was nice. I was able to enjoy my time with friends. I didn't feel overwhelmed to be out in public and encounter other mothers. When I saw a new mother, I felt joy for her. I would say a prayer for her and the child because I felt empowered to ask God to protect them.

I had imagined the years following my pregnancy to be so different. But I realized that although Charlotte wasn't physically present, she was spiritually present. She was enjoying her life in heaven; and, we were glad that she was in a place that was safer than any other.

Eventually, I had to clean Charlotte Evelina's room. Some things I left out, but I knew some things didn't need to be kept. I was comfortable putting away certain things because the feeling of depression and hurt wasn't there anymore. I cried while cleaning up her items but it wasn't tears of sorrow or pain. I cried because it was a chance for me to celebrate her life. I realized how much she was loved and if she had been alive, she would have had everything she needed and more.

We decorated her grave site for Easter. I really missed her on that day because I'd envisioned we would wear matching church dresses for that particular holiday. I felt it was only right to decorate her grave site with cute balloon bunnies and pinwheels to help with how I'd imagined she would have been – cute! I didn't feel sad decorating her grave site. I celebrated her life and Jesus' resurrection – everlasting life.

The most difficult holiday was Mother's Day. For a few days prior to it, I was nervous. I didn't really know how I would feel that day or how people would treat me. I hoped people wouldn't treat me with a lot of sympathy because I wasn't sad; and, I didn't need sympathy anymore. I almost didn't want to face society again but I encouraged myself by shifting my thoughts into positive affirmations. I kept Philippians 4:6-8 very close to my heart and mind:

> "Be careful for nothing; but in every thing by prayer and supplication with thanksgiving let your requests be made known unto God. And the peace of God, which passeth all understanding, shall keep your hearts and minds through Christ Jesus. Finally, brethren, whatsoever things are true, whatsoever things are honest, whatsoever things are just, whatsoever things are pure, whatsoever things are lovely, whatsoever things are of good report; if there be any virtue, and if there be any praise, think on these things."

It wasn't difficult to think positively because I had reached a point in my recovery where I was joyful and happy with life. On Mother's Day, people didn't show me any sympathy. People still wished me a 'Happy Mother's Day'. I quickly responded with gratitude and thanks.

On August 23, 2014, it was time to celebrate Charlotte Evelina's first birthday. We planned to release butterflies at her grave site because we wanted to show our daughter just how much she had transformed our lives. Our understanding of parenthood and love were enhanced spiritually because God had to teach us to love and have faith even when the ground falls from underneath you. We were overwhelmed with the number of family and friends that attended. We didn't really make it that big of an event but for those who did come, we were so appreciative. As we sang 'Happy Birthday' and songs of love to our daughter, I knew then my recovery was complete. I felt no more sorrow, depression, anger, frustration, or any negative feelings. I won this battle but I'm still fighting to win the war!

### My Testimony

I am full of joy, peace, happiness, gladness, and contentment. I am able to trust God again. My worship for God is strictly based on who He is and not what He's done. This battle helped me to not only overcome stillbirth but to help myself overcome insecurities and other strongholds I didn't know I had. I used the Bible as my resource to get through the battle. Day by day, I continue to talk to God and read His Word. I miss my baby everyday but I know she's in a magnificent place. My only goal now is to live accordingly to see her again in heaven.

### Personal Reflections

1. How are you recovering day by day?

2. What scriptures help to encourage you?

3. How do you know you are victorious?

# *Write It Out*

# Conclusion - To Mother An Angel

## *My Testimony*

I asked God, "Am I a mother?" Normal circumstances would define a mother by the various physical acts that a woman performs to care for her children. Growing up, I always considered a mother one who helps feed the children, clothe them, nurture them, encourage them, safeguard them, protect them, and discipline them. A mother is one who lives her life as an example for them. I asked God the question because based on my earlier experiences, I didn't fit my own definition of a mother. However, God answered me and said, "Yes, Latonia, you are a wonderful mother!" It shocked me when He said it because I didn't know why.

That's when God began to minister to me.

He let me know that few women can wholeheartedly live with the fact that their baby died. Few women can live normal day to day life knowing their child is not there. Even when a mother loses their child when the child is older, the reality of them being gone is unbearable at times. But there is one lesson that is reserved for certain mothers.

A select few are assigned to mother an angel.

It takes a special woman to face the world and declare they are a mother when the evidence isn't quite typical. This mother will still reference the child as though they are there. This mother will still carefully watch other children to ensure they are safe – even children of perfect strangers. This mother will celebrate and smile at other children when they accomplish great things. This mother will even be careful of her own actions because she knows her child is watching her from heaven. This mother knows that she has to acknowledge and accept Jesus Christ and live a life that is holy and pleasing to God because without these she won't see God in heaven. If she can't see God in heaven then that means she won't be able to see her angel who went before her.

Ever since Charlotte Evelina came into my life, it's been a rough but wonderful spiritual journey. The healing process of her stillbirth is further along now than it was when I first discovered her death. Her life has taught me about motherhood from a different perspective. I've always appreciated life because I'm a cancer survivor but now the appreciation for life is on a whole different level.

I love being a wife, a mother, a friend, a lover, a creative thinker, and whatever other 'hat' I have to wear throughout the week. On top of all that, I am a mother of a perfect angel! She had the perfect life. She wasn't abused or mistreated. She was able to laugh and enjoy life even in the confines of amniotic fluid. She had loving parents, grandparents, aunts, uncles, cousins, God-brothers, God-sisters, etc. She was beautiful! She will forever be my first baby girl!

I remember when we first found out we were pregnant, my primary request was I wanted God to get the glory. I didn't know what would be required but I'm glad He got and continues to get all the glory! I pray my testimony strengthens you during your journey.

### Personal Reflections

1. What has parenthood taught you?

2. What lessons did God help you to learn while going through a battle?

## _Write It Out_

# About the Author

Latonia Marie Price lives in Indianapolis, Indiana. She is married to Elder Iradel Price and is the youngest of four siblings. Latonia is an active member of Puritan Missionary Baptist Church and currently serves the ministry through various functions that allow her to demonstrate her leadership and passion for the Lord. She loves God and strives to live a life that is holy and acceptable to Him.

Latonia has a Bachelor of Science in Computer Information Technology and two Master's degrees in Computer Information Systems. She loves to read and do things that allow her to be creative (e.g. knitting, crocheting, weaving, painting, cooking, sewing, etc.)

In the coming years, she would love to venture away from the major technology world and perform more ministry work. She has acknowledged her calling as an evangelist and desires to write more books and speak around the world about how faith in God truly is the path to a better life.

*"Without faith, there's no hope, and without hope, we're just lost."* – *Latonia Price*

Printed in Great Britain
by Amazon.co.uk, Ltd.,
Marston Gate.